Sudden Dreams

SUDDEN DREAMS

NEW & SELECTED POEMS BY GEORGE EVANS

COFFEE HOUSE PRESS : : MINNEAPOLIS : : 1991

Grateful acknowledgment is made to the editors and publishers of the following publications in which many of these poems have previously appeared: *Conjunctions, Edge, Epoch, Figs, 5AM, Four by Four, Ironwood, Longhouse, New American Writing, Ninth Decade, Northern Lights, Oasis, Origin, Scripsi, Shearsman, Sulfur, Stand, Tenth Decade, The Threepenny Review,* and ZYZZYVA.

"Isaac," "Northern Island," "Pachinko King," "Study of My Father," and "The Dowser" were published in *Poetry.* "A Day," "Earl & Madge Take a Trip," "Punitive Damages," "To Who Said He Was Once a Painter," and "What It Is" were published in *New Directions in Prose and Poetry, 55;* "Eye Blade" in *New Directions in Prose and Poetry, 53;* "Saturday Towards Evening" in *New Directions in Prose and Poetry, 51.* "The Loss" appeared as a poster on the municipal bus systems of Atlanta, Chicago, Los Angeles, New York City, Oakland, San Francisco, and Washington, D.C., courtesy of TDI (Winston Network), as part of *Streetfare Journal.* "Ode to Fishers" was reprinted in *ARTS Review: National Endowment for the Arts,* Washington, D.C. "Isaac" was reprinted in *The Anthology of Magazine Verse and Yearbook of American Poetry* (Monitor Book Company, Inc., 1988).

Some of these poems also appeared in the following books published in England: *Nightvision* (Pig Press, 1983, 1984, 1988), *Wrecking* (Shearsman Books, 1988), and *Eye Blade* (Pig Press, 1988).

Author's Note: I wish to acknowledge the generous support of two Pre-Restriction-Era National Endowment for the Arts Creative Writing Fellowships, a Lannan Foundation Literary Fellowship, a California Arts Council Artists Fellowship for Literature, and a Japanese government *Monbusho* Research Fellowship for Literature.

The publisher thanks the following organizations whose support helped make this book possible: Elmer L. and Eleanor J. Andersen Foundation; The Bush Foundation; Dayton Hudson Foundation; Jerome Foundation; Minnesota State Arts Board; the National Endowment for the Arts, a federal agency; and Northwest Area Foundation.

Library of Congress Cataloging-in-Publication Data
Evans, George, 1948-
Sudden dreams : new & selected poems / by George Evans.
    p. cm.
ISBN 0-918273-86-2 : $8.95
1. Title.
PS3555.V216S8   1991   91-10107
811'.54 – dc20   CIP

Contents

Saturday Towards Evening

Nuclear Sonnet

Pachinko King

Fiddletown

Eye Blade

Horse on a Fence

for Lissa Gould

Saturday Towards Evening

Almost Perfect

The factory beats,
punching out parts.

No crickets no
birds. All night

in bed listening
to America

the baby grows
its bones expand

against darkness
it must explore

rocking with piston
strains upstreet

all night
barely crying.

A Summer

Tree limbs touch the water,
parts north swirl
around their tips

winding south, swimmers
going headfirst off the barges
except this one, slipping in

through branches
sucked by mill pipe
and current,

his hands flowering
from the river leaving
all on the bank to drown.

Working for the Iceman

He slams the ice down

small chips fly in your eyes

but melt before he smacks your head

for crying neon hums

bugs explode on lights & you pass chunks

to kids chasing the truck before he catches

on & Pleiades is up there the burlap

sacks he puts on his shoulder to hold the ice

flap in the wind the North Star the Bear

& Venus are out there

somewhere in the daylight & later

you'll shrivel & die

but now it's nothing now you're young

and believe he needs you.

The Scene

Jack roared his boozy breath
around the candles when the power was off

talking carpetbags at this date and pretties
adrift south by the tracks he was
a screamer, he was, slicing figures

with his arms
               balancing words
                          on his hands,

and his wife Tootsie said
her mama's coffee was so strong
you could ride it to St. Louis—

               there's a picture of her and her
               28 cats—scrawled on the back:

               Took 2 days to get 'em all in bows

Lightning

Jack was waked at Turbo's bar
                          some of the kids were all
for prying the lid to see
if he had pennies on his eyes the way someone said
but someone said
they did that to Lincoln
pennies were big then
what they'd heard was a joke
about putting pennies
in the fuse box when no one
had a fuse and there were plenty
electric jokes behind
Tootsie his wife's back
                          & Jack
stretched out like a wire
with his eyes burnt out
just wasn't around to get them
and there was the story of how he stole a couple flatcars
of copper on the Pennsy line & had to go down to B & O
to get away & then to get it like copper wire
hanging out the window of the engine
in the rain.

Study of My Father

The old man in the basement
shaking furnace ash
to get heat up this winter dawn
coughs—grunts spiraling in the ducts,
I cross each room to avoid him
coming up with chores, bells
from a Catholic church shake
factories in black air
strikers shrug and shuffle
heating their liquored bones.
My father the worker, the worked,
will not cross their line
but will not strike
believing both sides wrong,
will search this morning
for another job with his hands
which won't come clean
even two days out—
he grabs and slices the bread:
This is the only jewel, he says,
ruffles my hair, sends me
with a shovel into the snow.

Note

Late at night
night roars,

trees bend
and are beasts.

Sits a mother
sits a father

listening
to wind

round corners
on their table,

staring
at a new world

weighted
with a spoon:

I'll be back,
I swear I will,

next time, next
life, maybe.

The Atomic Soldier

A great dust falls on 1956 Nevada where he's young
and lusty enzymes pop. The bomb stands up behind him
after rushing from the bunker for a shot, a flower
on his head. Everyone is learning to dance,
storming the moment, and history is wind
sweeping one-store towns and celebrations.
Ponytails bounce, brown-bagged gin swings around
black & white Nevada, and flamingo pink casinos
float like islands on the sand.

Decades later his bones glow
on the verge of bursting forth, and he melts
into a floral-patterned easy chair before the ghost,
his thyroids gone, nursing a beer, trying to make football
important, and wind is rising, and fog on the ice
plant in California where he drifts and nods
into a dream of blinding desert blooms
planted in a dancing and a storm.

Wrecking

The nails pop,
redwood ripping, plaster

rattles,
ribbing burst to light

125 years later
pipes dropping

to the basement; roof
lifting, hovering, crashing

to the yard; history, all of it
crashing we can't breathe the air

dense, scarlet, tearing
this thing with bars and saws

in the 20th century
on the 3rd floor smashing glass

watching the fogged
city as it sprays

hitting ground by plate and sliver,
thinking of god, and of Hoffer, longshoreman,

fingers crushed, standing
near a piano wanting to play,

and of tiny black bananas sold in Spanish
on a clear day

in places where the world comes down
by the second.

Saturday Towards Evening

1 :

Switches hit low
riding Dodge & Ford
humping, young men
in hairnets,
shirts buttoned to the neck —
girls in black lipstick,
dark purpled cheeks,
eyeliner back to their ears:
Promenade & Spanglish
back, forth, around,
rap sound
bone-deep loud.

2 :

The Chat & Chew:
white saucers and coffee,
hamburgers on the grill
like Cadillacs,
waitresses grim so foul a pit
what do, one of them asks,
you want you
son of a bitch?

3:

La Santaneca de la Mission
next to Sophia's Pizza,
glitter and throb, Pioneer
Chicken its windows wide
salt & oil of the sea
biting the air spicing it
Chinese King's Panadería
its lights on in the back
cleaning up: mah-jongg tiles
and Latin music click.

4:

As darkness comes
TV flickers above the bar
in Carlos' Club,
a risen moon,
a lady walks her baby
outside waiting on the sidewalk—
jukebox wails,
it glitters in smoke
these are good times
where the sun drops
leaving no scar
where it goes.

Mission, San Francisco

The Dresser

Bumping chairs, lamps, crushing
extension cords in nap I go
barefoot to the tools spread there:

a continent, a body.
Callused hands brushing ear
and finger jewelry too small

to grip just touch and knock
about looking down. A tiny land.
What do I know,

believed for bullshit, love,
position, truth rarely
this world so tamed

it sets gold and near-gold
by a mirror
believing it doubled.

Why should you believe
anything. You
should not. Come into

the field. Look. At
the paintbrush the click
beetle the face

you decorate
do not decorate
from fear.

Isaac

I sit in the light of my father's house.
All that's over, what went between us.
To be sacrificed, even the thought of it,
is insane, but we can live with anything—
change friends, desires, change what we covet
in our father's house, and live with anything.

In guilt there is no middle ground, in guilt
the mind revolves upon deception. Waste.

We went together to the sea and at the sea
watched sailboats tack a cold expanse.
The fact of life, he said, is that we change
each other, change, and never are the same.
Regard the shift and tend the sea
that each idea and man must cross alone.

Marriage

Not one thing
not anyone the moon
is high in cedar high
in unnamed trees
branching the fence
a web
between here and there—

we alone by house
or occupation alone
by choice by force of emotion
are something something rattles
we are taken to a space
where it dissolves, a second
or year later, the self.

The Times

Light collects
in the eyes to

itemize
perpetuate

and live
even

tenaciously
indifferent.

*

Out of the avalanche
comes beauty, another
land to endure.

*

Going north
to duck squawk

land flashes
from the side,

bird flocks speck
the yarrow and fallen

trees, holding
to little.

*

Love is fire
like a branch
birds land on

turning it actual,
rooted, a tree
of the heart

they enter
to be consumed,
we've come

to think
by flames
and live in wood.

Northern Island

An absence of things and water
around the island make it live.

The beauty of winter trees
is that they'll change,
not that they are barren.

Like the island beach, the mind
returns to each spot, wandering
as it always must

the beginning and end
of two worlds.

Ode to Fishers

It is caught in grass,
in loaves of bread,
by shallow lines in the hand.

We must stand and admire
the various types of hooks
in this world.

And sponge. Forget not boats
crossing water like words
in deafness: wasting, unheard

striking no land.

They learn the passions
of nothingness.

When food is everywhere
the nets alone still hunger.

Nuclear Sonnet

Nuclear Sonnet

Zero zone
zone in hell
substantial nothing death trip zone

the denim, the leather, the smoke
zone
where nothing is written or said which is sensible
sensate zone

incapable of guilt or its brother murder
zone
moving away from description
                              decision

and the head which fears   originality
                              but lives   for its discovery
as if by accident

scrapes its own flesh raw
its own raw flesh

against everything .
                    .

                    .

                    .

Nuclear free ozone zone
                         neon blue calligraphy of Tokyo zone
wolf zone
            purple blood of the heart zone
                                             marble
                                             rock
                                             and ripped off testicle
                                             war
                                             zone

passion colored miraculous bandaged birth zone

zone of the heart on fire
                    of the flaming haired woman

                              the flaming boned man zone

          who mistake these cities for their own

Bond

She struggles with her baby in the rain   water drumming
   the buggy hood
                           dropping a glassy net on her face

her simplicity   such strength and focus of motion   beauty

   and grace

                  I imagine her naked   streaming   glistening

with rain as only a man can imagine

                                 or perhaps she is one who prefers

her own and is finished with men   relentless love

                  near the hawthorn tooth in its dark shrub

   where she hovers   rain bouncing   on her watch   holding

                  her arm like a wing

reminding me of my mother   who asked one promise

      for what she had done: to try to grow old

      which centuries later I fell in love and understood

What It Is

Crossing the snow line we walk a white bridge
arched and frozen over rushing rivers
if we fall we'll be sucked in
to mountains or snow,
sucked into distant
light.

Similar things
happen at the track, you bet

                    a longshot
            no good
beautiful

losing horse then wind up
weaving traffic home

but hit nothing though you stopped at the Turf Club
for a stiff one and float into freeway space
thinking I am of another time, it's *not*
yesterday, certainly not today but
mainly all that is yet to happen.

                    for Bill Barich

Punitive Damages

The owl rises

hooking black air rises

apart from everything   scandal, love, electricity

and all that

        following blood shades

by wind-lift, drought, fire, shotgun and divorce

over mountain bones of earth
face spread
across darkness plucking mice from the field
changing air
from an acre to a mile
the owl pounds air then glides
its beginning and end
this bird which is no bird this lightning
                         crack and splinter
appears as contour on the skin
which is also lightning
and has been from the instant of mother's pain

breathing life into the storm
and earth   its poverty and grace
                 where only traces

     electrical branches   crack the dark

exploding underground   under skin where an owl maneuvers

alone

endlessly

rushing nowhere
                with purpose   while I'm jumping

ribbon tracks towards Ohio, Georgia, Idaho maybe, rocking
by wallboard shacks
which pass for the great house of America
with radio sounds, music rising
chicken bone rattle
rattle
goes a bastard with tire chains in the corner
of the car and says come here you little white
slick as a wet chicken
skin motherfucker
gonna show you
gonna make you,
                            but I fly over the great continent
breaking his eye slashing
at other tramps with half a pool cue on the railroad while I
    dream,
throwing one off near San Antonio
because he didn't understand about what is small
is miserable and death itself if you prod it worse
if you make size the issue
riding America
following electric blood
reading Bo signs on cars and fences
blood in leaves
and the sound of iron scars
rib by rib where I first was last
breaking my own heart under moonlight
where a great owl floats
without family
and I slave without shame for bread

Equinox Zydeco

First day of summer   cusp   and born with a callus

on my heart
          rolled between spirit fingers

            which would seem strange

even the sound strange
            to name—

my eyes their fingerprints,

traces of light on cosmos pitch,

my tongue their sarcasms

           which won't allow comfort

but I wake up over and over

           streaming,

sliding through emptiness,

        filling it

with light and darkness   and with my bones

fill space

           which will be memory

To Who Said He Was Once a Painter

I remember things like times the electric

   got switched off plunging us into darkness

   we lit nickel candles then made it

   on the rug those were times which inform

   the very sound of land yes and I

   wouldn't let her go for any thing or one

   but she did go and I will say

   and always   that was

where I built the road

by what I know   listening all night

and listening all day

to love's commotion

Continued

The birds are gone . . . reality . . . elsewhere

where

dinosaur prints rise with Columbus Avenue

cobbles stuck out from churning car

traffic

     and whistle   from the graveyard

where what is lost was king

and what was king has gone.

What I Meant Was This

The moon crushed everything
ruined the whole deal

but one wants friends who speak with both desires to be heard

and the fear they will be

making it worth

the light which surrounds us

in its many forms   and histories

A Day

It is a filled bowl, a wide-angle San Francisco from the streetcar
   above Delores Park and my wife has quit work to go to school
   to become a teacher and bought a new pair of shoes
   but we seem quite happy in the poorhouse

Iranians are streaking the Straits of Hormuz on motorboats
   loaded with nuclear weapons and switchblades,
   but the bombs won't work because Iran has no plutonium—
   I admire such determination wishing we were all plowing
   around rivers and oceans on water skis or rafts merely wishing
   to get even
               then visions of holocaust interrupt:
visions of oppression, grief, terror and everything difficult
about life (such as rent, direction, purpose, meaning) are all
erupting like human-sized volcanoes, though I'm suppressing
it for the sake of looking at the sky, looking at a man on the car
looking at me who resembles a friend of many years
I used to run into on streetcars after work and take home,
who is now dead from AIDS, and I can't stop looking,
though I know he is dead and suddenly
would like to see him more than anything
take him home, whip on some Texas Blues, Lightning,
throw a chicken in a pot or roll burritos
and joints so the three of us
  —our friend, my new shoed wife and I—
can go crazy and call up everyone we know to come over
which we do, and they do
                    suddenly I would like to see him
again and will suppress anything to believe it's possible it is
a typical day because I'm always suppressing one thing
or another for the sake of something and am yet
to hook into the notion that life is irreversibly
terrible, difficult and should be enjoyed as terrible
and difficult because the fact is that it is not,

though I am open, and work to be open,
very open in spite of distractions
and all the fears of distractions

Just give me an anesthetic, my brainpan aches,
    my hidden tumors ache, my histories are aching why
    do I like it pure and untrammeled—my testicles, no my
    balls are aching my cock is aching my eyes my hair
    my fingernails: aching and I seem to like it because one day
    I want to wake up to a terrible world which will be my element
    and all the bombings murders lies and hellstorms and lost
    friends be home sweet home
    if I could only be miserable
    and like what is happening

Otherwise it's a typical day and I pay no attention to that
    which will crush and concentrate instead upon fruitstands
    in the Mission, memories of strolling Manhattan
    in a dream state entranced by everything the homeless the
    hustlers the suits and all the women
    who thrill me as no man could   I wouldn't lie
    even as social amenity about that about wanting them all
    it's not the uppermost thing in my mind
    but it is something

Then I bang open double slab doors on tube hinges
    after now a terrible day and drink tiny glasses of beer
    between trips to telephone booth
    sized urinals glazed with cracks like fine pottery
    sitting with my friend in my head his curly hair
    speckled   haloed white
    from painting a house after two mornings
    in a coffee shop avoiding it
    feeding the jukebox jerking
    other customers around amusing

specifically unhappy waitresses
I weigh the virtues
of seeming gauche with notions but no real knowledge
about everything and saying so even then
not knowing he would die for his pleasures
or I would survive for mine, that a choice was made
finally against something
but being made for something
and that he would be as irreplaceable as an eye

for Tony (Scott) Pfafflin

Snake Year

Rivulet   spilling over sheared mountain
        where road cuts through   a rivulet itself
winding to the sea winding

                my eyes back and forth over it
like a screw's thread down to the sea—

it's become impossible to pay attention to any one thing,
I've tried
            am trying now
                        but fail to separate the world
into worlds
                even years into days   each one fluid

slipping away as it starts   for the future

                no one understands
what's coming
                but we manage this accord
                with what seems now

to be sliding at us down the mountain

                                                1/1/89

Pachinko King

Uji

Fires rock with the current.
I keep coming, staring up river
from Uji Bridge, where Hideyoshi
hanged some fool with a bucket
by the ankles
to get water midstream for tea,

when they are fishing, each man
a dozen cormorants on spruce reins
whirling and diving
like wind-up birds
only hungry,

fires blazing on the boats
as lures, hulls banging
together sparks flying fish
so desperate some leap ashore to escape

the way one goes sometimes
crazy to stay alive.

And the birds: if the first one in's not the first one out
and the second the second, they refuse to work;

bands on their throats
keep them from swallowing
all but the smallest fish,
yet they go after the big ones
which makes them like men.

Finally when the moon's up & the crowd
drunk, their arms linked shouting on shore,
or singing on excursion boats strung with *Asahi*
lanterns, chewing squid on sticks and chucking cans,

I get caught up in the mountains up river
and wonder how many there are
who never return to sea.

A Renaissance Drunk

They never read their Hedylos, nor could,
where he sings how sweet was Sokles
in his cups, how he wrote better for it,

or the sot Santōka:

The leaves drop   (horohoro)
weaving down drunk
from their trees

                      Beauty.
                      I am the leaves.

The shape of the traveler
in the puddle is the traveler
                      or in the wine,

walking, balancing a dragonfly
on his hat,

threading, stepping lightly
over shadows in the pines.

Pachinko King

He sits all day in the great palace
thumbing, launching his silver balls,
pacheen, pacheen, straight up, and they bounce
back down through a pin forest
racking points, flushing silver balls
from a chute into cans stacked around him,
until he's done and rises

to trade his balls for pens,
watches, cigarettes, lighters,
and struts down an alley to trade
again through a tiny window for cash
in patent leather shoes, see-through
socks so his tattoos show, bag pants,
bowling shirt, and high-shouldered coat.

The Capital is steaming, neon sizzles,
paper doors rattle and slide, disheveled
whores in *kimono,* cheek makeup streaking,
hair askew, bristled with plastic combs,
dot the street without sidewalks, and smile
for the devil of love, the king who comes
walking, wearing his skin like a dream.

Japan

at Ryōanji

In this land
I cannot sleep—

swallows fanning
the edge of the roof,

pines wired
to perfection,

and the sun with a place
it *must* rise in the garden.

Rocks scattered by caliper
hold my mind in the great rock garden

it is hard to feel
faultless in perfect moss

everything fine, all things
exquisitely small.

But what in my own land
speaks without fabrication—

only death, and death
has nothing to do

with a wild flower
ruffling

by a carefully broken fence
splitting

with its petals
what's not to be seen:

the wind, pouring out,
the wind.

4 2

At Shinbashi: New Bridge

A blossom: a flame
along   the eye

a bridge   a world
one sees

reflected   crossing

those
flowers   there

his shadow.

    *

Dreams have course,
the man not the man

reflected is talk.
What holds is manner.

    *

The bridge lies cross
to wind and the shoe

cross that with it
would go against

the flow as all will
who would make it.

Nara

In late spring I rattle
on the milk train to Nara
the windows dropped: hot air stink,
diesel, manure blowing from the paddy fields,
stopping at every village and semblance of village
baking, fans screwed to the ceiling make it worse
on my second beer bought from a vendor running
beside us I stare at a box lunch looking like a Mondrian
balanced on my knees—it also looks like a topological map
in a box, or a picture puzzle I can't decide which the manure
is so intense I stow it and concentrate on school kids packed
in with me off to visit the ancients, see the giant Buddha
in the biggest building in the world and get our pockets
chewed by deer in the deer park, then they start poking me,
chanting: *Tengu, Tengu!* (fire-red, long-nosed goblin)
touching my beard, asking how Mickey Mouse is doing,
and using an accent perfected watching samurai films
I grunt: *Getting fat! Growing a beard!*
which stuns them
                    then they explode
and we are bouncing to Nara to see the ancients,
excited, discussing America in Mickey Mouse voices
when taking my third beer from the runner
I see long yellow threads
pinned to their school shirts:
red dragonflies, tied by the waist
on loops, which flutter in the car
tearing themselves apart
to fly away.

The Emperor's 79th Birthday

Shortwave in the kitchen:

boat telegraphy: Hong Kong
Russia   Borneo   Seoul,

animals drowning in waves.

Spring morning,
peacocks yowling
in the park.

Flowers in a gray vase
by the door
alive all week.

Purple flowers.

Rumors of war.

Dancers

Strands of hair on a chalk-white neck,

bells, incense, eyelids painted red,

a mirror made of flowers their feet

beat and spin, streams of *kimono*

flow on the path we are walking together

in fumes of the moon, string music

washing us like rain, a white umbrella:

at Arashiyama a full moon tonight.

Kyōto

The Missing Sunflower

The bombing continues   little wooden buildings dissolve

disintegrated from the sky   that best frame for spring

and for the willows arching their green canes touching

the ribbon rivers

the cherries pink

smoke rising   Nagasaki

and the sunflower melt

                curl

                   turn crisp

                          collapse

Van Gogh would be pleased it had traveled

and so far   but would a man who built a canvas

          as much as painted one   care   if it hung

in a building   being its own building   own shelter

and dwelling after all

             sunlight hitting it

                     dropping

while Japan itself falls apart

on the plains as on canvas   curling and shivering with fire

In Asia

1 :

The carp are young
for a moment
their fat bodies
wild

from the moon
falls design from

distance comes
a world

2 :

On the teacup a
star on the radio

men reduce their towns

wires hum in the wall
behind

the flowers each leaf

like unemployed friends
so perfectly arranged

3:

Catamites at court
come at last to think it grand

being used their black

polished teeth
dance about the pond

4:

A woman whipping tea,

though disorder seems
our state and blood latent

in wooden poles
around the room beyond her

oiled hair about
to burst

       (television in the corner,

        the wood and paper
        room cluttered
        with junk,

        moon streaming through
        its dark,

        baseball scores
        from next door)

the tea is perfect

Ryōkan as an Old Man

Bones are pine
their elbows crook
and nothing straight
but the trunk
where it's rooted is stable.

Birds darting
without concept
of difference in earth or sky
are pure motion.

The dawn bell
counts men
and leaves.

A wave,
another,
water rashed
against stone —

behind my shoulder
a wave

and then a dream.

Fiddletown

Fiddletown

In Fiddletown the dogwoods bloom,
wildflowers cloud the rusting knots
of car parts and appliances in weeds.

You can lean a chair
in the street and watch infinity
stream by, catkins curl, bug zip,

or Gold Rush buildings drop
nail by nail into nothing.
If something hits you you

know why, and if not you know why.
Bird cannons bang the orchards
but birds keep drilling fruit,

sorting idle threats from the rest,
heat dancing in strings
on asphalt where lizards streak

twisting their knobs in sun
until evening and the giant
fiddle bolted down to Fiddletown

Community Club and all the porches
squeak. It's pathetic
how outside town they want everything

electric, fit, smooth as highway
through rock crust and Chinese walls
stacked one cent the foot any height

like a bad, beautiful dream stitching
red dirt hills, while all they ever say
is there used to be gold up here.

The Loss

Screen door bangs gravel leaps
car spins out.

You won't hit me again —
I'm better than that.

He knew it. She could get
a deer from the kitchen window
in total dark. Make ice cream.
Strip a frog leg. Bowl.

And nobody liked
him better.

Revelation in the Mother Lode

I walk into the vineyard at night, into acres of cordoned vines
    against their stakes at pruning time, but see, stretching
    off through tule fog, only cross-marked graves.

How did it come to be that my generation would be stiff
    under hoarfrost, and that I should come across them
    twenty years after watching them die to remember and feel
    I've truly wasted my time, have left no mark upon the earth
    in their name, have left only the small craters of a boot
    sucking vineyard mud.

And is this guilt, or the product of being swept up
    in a time on human earth when few do more than raise
    the cause of their own names — and am I one, or is all this
    death just sloth which one pretends
    to work against the belly of
    but which in fact
    controls?

You who return to me as vines in the deep night under fog
    have come at a bad time, a time when the world is obsessed
    with rubbing you smooth, and its concentration
    on ceremony brings you to nothing.

Somewhere, mixed in with all the rest I'd meant to get to
    which is receding, is a day floating above jungle, flak
    exploding in small fists from the trees, rocking
    the chopper where I sit in shock and blood and urine
    staring into patchwork fields.

I stand behind bamboo shaking, thinking of Nguyet
    in a Saigon bar, worried how willingly we forget,
    bombs dropping like hair straight down   a shadow
    a black sheet   everything about us muscle   hot
    prick and resolve   and have no idea where I am

but am everywhere   and she   wobbling on spiked heels
around the bar stools and smoke has everything I cannot
not the least of which is a reason
                              which makes her more beautiful
than possible, but also quite a bit like the ragged edge
of a ruined wall, and like the crisp brown bamboo leaves
dropping after terrible heat, dripping with an ache I love
which is more for youth than anything   certainly not war,
which also feels like dropping.

How tired I am of hearing about that war,
    which one should struggle
    to keep the nightmare of, suffer from rather than forget.
    I don't want to heal, and am sick of those who do.
    Such things end in license.

Back here it turns out newspapers
    and monuments are taxidermy;
    there is little retribution, little learning; what is lost
    is forgotten; sometimes it gets so bad I'm not sure
    I'm the one who lived . . . then come upon you in a field
    —a one-time soldier with a trick knee, flagging humor,
    monsoon debt—and find you enfolded by fog as if by spirits,
    and become the visage of all that's been
    thrown from the world.

The Dowser

It's witching weather.
Twigs in the high trees snap.
It's wind gets up there, wind gets anywhere.

But the world sifts down and reaches back.
Rippled stream and flat water both
get shape by what goes on below —
a water tension — the way a face

gets shaped by what's inside, the way eyes look.
You know what's in there, you can tell
lies from affection.

The world is, everything is,
geology, and a right-cut stick
or charm on a chain finds it all.
Soon or late, everything goes down.

A Tenant Helps

I'll tell you what:
I been up and down every track and trail in this canyon
and ain't seen one thing yet like what you call

   PRISS-TEEN.

Never did like that word.

When I look at that forest
all I think about's the pain I'd get
if I had to stump it.

Y'all come up here with a head full of gimme
and bullshit, but don't know a bear from a squirrel.

I'm a squash grower myself,
and grow squash bigger than any one of you
bent over double like
if I hauled off and kicked you in the gut.

Farmer Song

The crops might wither, maybe
earth will, chaff blow, air
blur with seed sweet Jesus
till nothing's clear,

but where we've been won't change,
what we've done stays done—
like a plow pulled over fields
brings new earth, so the sun.

Country Western Bar

Look what the cat drug in.

You're crawlin in my eyes,
blockin light as the sun sets, son—
time's a droppin heat on its way to zero,
and I'm across that old country line.

Around here we hang folks
for lookin cross-eyed at dogs, Ritzo,
and bear lies about long enough to breathe.
Fella dressed like you never had his heart broke.
So screw you and the horse you rode in on, Slim.

As I was sayin when this hog on ice walked in:

Gimme another beer, Fatso,
and next *MAN* comes in
give him one too.

Stream

Because it is there and I can walk along it   unmolested
unquestioned at midnight
                             watching the coyote slink in full
moon against silver, weaving its way down the slope nervous
that I'm there
                   but intent upon motion and water   nosing
burrows, looking up   coming because it is there because
the rushing is there like the sound of wind through trees
leading its silence
               leading its thirst
                          wider than white Sierras
above the hills, and what can it care, what can the coyote care
that I stink of diesel or tobacco or the emptiness
the emptiness what can it care
                      that I've dreamed myself
into every state, driven myself into every state, paid my way,
worked my way, begged my way, screamed and prayed,
               forced and found
my way into every state, what can the coyote care   moving
over the skin of earth towards water
                     with its padded feet,
its claws, its white teeth built to reflect the light of air
and hold its sweating tongue, and its hair to carry its halo
what can it care
              that I stand in the moon stock-still
without fur, without purpose except what I invent,
             without hope
of slithering over earth's face, running, jumping naked in air
over it   self-propelled   through the cold cold
all night   once   without dying   what can it care

The Poet

My favorite thing's Rock & Roll.
No shame in that. I crush cars at the yard,
like to watch em shrink; glass cracks and flies,
you never seen such a thing. Handles pop,
bang, and sometimes you see em circle the yard,
and sometimes you don't—that's this scar here.

I'm the one they call *poet.*
I ain't no poet. Springsteen, Dylan . . . now
there's poets: pop strings, dance a bit,
say what you want and make a mint.
Well I ain't one.

Did this song up to the Odd Fellows dance one night?
I ain't doin it again, but that's when they put it on me.
I wouldn't mind if it got me some once in a while,
but it don't. I put up with it since it someday might.

It means two things:
you do Rock & Roll,
or know something they don't.

That's me on the end
there in that picture
at the softball picnic on the wall—
the one with the balls.

Molester

You put a bad thing in the air, buddy,
more than a wrong thing, jick,
and when that last horn cranks,
when that cosmic blitz gets set
to stretch you out,
you'll think about it then,

but too late
and too bad, buddy,

you're a town off on your own,
south end of a northbound horse,

and one day it's going to hit you, buddy,
you won't feel so good about it, sweetie,

when nobody comes to see you off
but flies and a boiling sun.

Earl & Madge Take a Trip

Cut every coupon and used every one.
Saved everything, even soap bits,
and didn't waste money on the lottery
which anyway Earl calls tax for the stupid.
Then we joined a travel club and went to Hawaii
(still caint *believe* that's part of this continent!), Hong Kong
where they shop all day and we spoke the language,
Bangkok where they got hundreds of filthy rivers and air
that you caint breathe but the cutest little kids, and . . .
well, I caint recall where all, but then — and get this — we
went to Japan for godsakes. Well I'm here to tell you,
Tokyo's one big pinball machine, but that Kyoto's the cutest
little thing . . . and all those people . . . they got Japanese
everywhere, just everywhere! They like us though.
They ought to, we keep em in noodles as Earl says.
Anyway, then they flew us down to Nagasaki for free
cause they're trying to build up the tourists, you know.
I caint hardly begin to tell you what all, but
that place used to swarm with Christians?
They made a big point to show us the churches, and museums
filled with Christian things (they killed them all
of course, so all they *got* is things), but you know what?
I never *will* forget where they dropped that bomb.
Early one day they took us to a park and said:
There it is; that's the place.
And there it was, no bigger than your eye.
I looked up at the sky, and I looked down at that dot . . .
well I still caint believe it. And they were so nice!
Earl said: "You're gonna always be nice to somebody
can drop all *that* shit on a little dot."
I maybe might agree, but aint slept right since.
Come over the house. I'll show you things *you* won't believe.

What the Neighbor Said

Big crops attract attention.
Better to keep sparse and steal
from the store, he said, *a body*
can't get by on work alone in this mess
not worth a bucket of piss or window
to throw it out, and politicians useless
as tits on a bull, then nailed up his place
and moved on.

But somebody's got to grow it,
somebody's got to grin on the way
to the bank. He was thick above the neck,
wouldn't take help, bone-skulled proud,
sending his girls off and old woman,
then going to San Francisco with a whore
and whiskey bottle, to hang himself
from shower pipes, a family man
and dirt farmer who couldn't make the tax,
hung there like a rag, water dripping
on his shoes — damned fool, twisting there
silly, his tongue blue, the beet color
gone from his face.

Blood Sport

Off a wine drunk in Plymouth each July
when the County Fair comes he gets work
as Forty-Niner, to pan, hoot, and make sure
everyone calls the place Pokerville
like it should be and was before some Babbitt
scared by poker peeled the shine, deballed it,
and called in the trailer parks.

Water swishing in a pie pan filled with sand and fish
sinkers painted gold, stands the Hope of Pokerville,
the Amador Bomber, face like an old wheelbarrow,
fists as big as bull's nuts, known in his prime
as the Gold Dust Kid, sneered at as the Pyrite
Piss Ant, there he stands: defiant and
defiant, the undiscovered end of time,
too old, too nuts to call Bingo, but standing
like manzanita, gnarled, red, hard to uproot,
with the moon and sun in his eyes,
looking up, throwing hooks
at the sky.

The Weather in Amador

The Cooper's hawk sits on a live oak
twisting its head, scanning for mice,
for crossing birds, observing shade,
intensifies essentials, keeps slight attention
on the rest, drops and disappears to reappear
on a distant tree — all afternoon pinning a grid
with its shadow, clearing the field it sweeps
the land into silence except for wind.

Eye Blade

In the years after the war earth kept shaking. Landscapes
shifted, windows shattered. It was unpopular to be unpopular.
Strong words disappeared like bees into hives. Films were made,
songs written, clubs formed, monuments erected. Objects slipped
in and out of the sacred, in and out of the picture. Everyone paid
to wait to get in then paid again and maybe got in. Cliffs dropped,
mills shut, pots fell from windows, cars from bridges, hearts fell
like coins through grating—earth kept shaking, wind rising.
Weapons replaced gods, instruments people, TV replaced distance
and the mind. The missile lines grew long, long, long
as a child's breath long.

Air hazed by seed and bug, arms heavy
after work he sits, denting a can with his thumb
on the steps of the house which owns him
watching a figure inch uphill across the valley.
Skateboards scrape, spark, evening news begins
its tally, its explosions, the world exploding
block by block towards him, thing so large
the whole will not be seen.

Up blacktop as up a wall the figure climbs
cobblestone knuckled street toting a sack.
San Francisco glitters in a circle below.
Hunchbacked splinter on a hill, inebriate
wandering, bottles clanking, moving but still:
dot, insect, man, instrument, subject.

A shadow. It peels and approaches
gathering shape: edges emerge,
throwing-star whizzing, it grows,
wheels away dragging its shadow—
a hawk, holding the world
in its eye: an island.

A blind man, stick tapping, stops, jerks,
rapping, tap
          tap, fishing, reaching, scraping
ahead, edge against edge, feeling the world
through his stick, the whole black sphere
attached to its tip.

A child in the shape of a bowl.
A powdered form, body striped with ribs,
eating dust without protest
in forced geophagy, eyes shut,
no world beyond its plain
littered with blanket shacks.
Stone. Ripened fig. Speck in the cosmos.
Pair of eyes like planets.

A black mark bouncing through forest
leaps over root and vine, ferns snapping
between her toes she runs from a village
whose life is food, who longs for the north
with its malls, who covets abstract visions
of Texas, hears gunfire and looks back thinking
of a water pot on her table flowering as it bursts,
and of TV, if its figures, like water, are stored within.

A farmer marching to a cadence beyond the trees,
chanting, fluting, shirt frayed, dissolving through hills
to revolt, to reach the capital grown in him like a fist,
ignorant of what he'll face: that everyone wants control,
and no one wants control—
what everyone really wants is money.
His voice is smaller than a pin's tip, a bird's beak
drilling air, waving its words like a flag,
a target lighting its center.

The figure moves deeper away through the hills
wandering mapless, sighting blue and gray
peaks to measure how far, or remember nothing
is far, everything far: arriving isn't the point,
the point is to move not away from or to,
but constantly in the place where the mind centers,
driving it through mountains.

The road becomes a dot. Red-winged blackbirds
stick to the wires then explode across the field.
He's walking in extreme states through the landscape.
The beauty is painful. He recognizes long-denied voids
spanned or camouflaged for love or attention. He's stuck,
confused between grief and self-pity, knowing patience
can turn to bitterness and vanity greed, but what
of aimlessness and sentimental ruth which have
become his sack, and what of the journey
which has become his destination?

The poet Tu Fu, grain of dust to China,
watching chaos cross the horizon, pain
real and imagined, pities himself, hair
too thin to tie back, wanting his art
to bring fame, lost in the dead Li Po
drowned grabbing the moon where it blazed
like a white leaf past his boat, Li Po,
who drunk could make a ragpicker king.

Its nature is that it's outside, outside the outside.
Not a vehicle but a motion. No meaning, no correlative,
no use, no rejection, no acceptance, no form, no intention,
no morality, no religion, no school, no forebears, no
value, no price, no time, no bones. It is its own
future and purpose, own audience and shill.
It has no nature. It has the world.

Plowing uphill the runner blurs
the world, losing sense of the motionless, everything
moves: islands of flattened gum, discarded fruit,
exploding paper, statues jumping on lawns,
fences and clouds stream by. No distinguishing
what's forced to move from what itself is moving,
every speck of the world falling apart,
gathering, falling apart.

A mockingbird in its tree, long tail flicking:
guitars, cork pop, telephone, jackhammer, nail
squealed from wood, snoring. Creature of sound:
door squeak, hose spray, cop whistle, siren, jazz:
picks what has passed and sings back
over power line, building, car: voice
of the times on a twig, rocking,
returning what won't be had.

The wall, the black wall rising. Dead list
in the capital, black list, stone mirror
faces float across searching its columns,
names to touch, lean upon and fall through
into space. Rolling stone which will not roll.
Wound which doesn't close except in sleep.
Numbers small for war though somehow less
forgivable perceived as error, though all
battle is error. And when its shine dulls,
sting fades, and those who weep go dry,
what good will be a wall?

An orchid in light
its veins are bones
the world is mad we
live on air unwinding
and resist the dark
but touch the dark
for death's the stem
and root, impatient
growling thing.

Bosatsu of a thousand whirling arms,
windmill on a hillside, each arm an event,
skill, perspective: world of a thousand
eyes viewing a thousand things at once
and each thing equal; world of a thousand
windows opened on as many things meaningless
one by one as there are self-obsessions;
the world which will not tolerate one view.

The obsessed turning in circles, gathering
chips as if this is Reno and somebody wins:
I'll take one of those, one of those, and
one of those. The rest of you take a hike,
get fucked, bug off, hit the road, corpse—
this is my movie, this is me and me me me.

The Master said, getting up from where
he'd been kicked across the casino through
sawdust into a corner under a slot machine:
It's a bridge, all road and no sidewalk.
Don't fall asleep.

A flying ant crawls over an ash, stops,
washes its wings then goes on, lives to live,
exceeding neither limits nor potential,
excoriating nothing in its pursuits.

A boy in a tree at night above Main Street,
Peru. Below, a woman with a sack of sugar
on her head waddles to a traffic light and waits.
He has entered the world of the dead, and hears
drums on the ground below, drums lined up in rows,
each with a drummer: enemies of the Inca,
gutted then stretched in a smokehouse
until their stomachs are taut, fit
to drum through the jungle.

Inches above water the osprey hangs,
then dropping locks its talons in,
but the fish is strong, heavy,
and drags it into the liquid sky
through rings of impact down
to silence.

An old woman wobbles up, air bending
as she bends, wind pushing her down,
each moment stops, each step
an arrival she takes the hill
hobbling, teetering and suffers
the incurable: her skin.

A clump of weeds breaks the pavement
throwing lower worlds to light.
The rough the unwanted struggle most
but last by the effort, translating
land into landscape, revolting
underfoot. Things which are deep
and will not be cut.

Sparks fly from a guitar
player's fingers in a Chuck Berry duckwalk
across the skyline, wind shears
him, wind harp blown to life
on a high ridge culture dances,
twists, the passions course,
blood pounds and words drop
like hammer blows. Rock & Roll.

It's the specter of death. More than a cloud, a second
sky; Rangda, breasts like hanging knee-socks, shaking
her ass, whipping a trance on reason, stabbing the world
in full view of the world; Kali, popping her cheeks
like a drum, dangling life by its skin, flaying,
peeling the planet, palms out, hips in frenzy,
watching the world blow apart
as if on a screen.

In slo-mo the column rises into a ball, sweeping
cows from their fields, babies from cribs, hands
from their bodies, charring wallpaper, melting
the fence: no more flowers, trees or lawns, no more
houses, cars, or baseball. No more music, no more
sex, books, computers, airplanes, insects and birds
a vapor, elephants fried to a crisp, whales thrown
aloft: the reverse of the world.

A voice struggles to be heard,
but which mechanism detects it as a lie,
and how is it recognized? Patience
is the power of the eye, naïveté
skill when it comes to observing men
not given to truth, as silence is skill
in the wilderness, watching. A spot,
a mirror in light among mirrors, the eye.

Off your high horse, mister.
Yours is no profession or branch,
and you no bird to piss down
on fields and peasants, there are
peasants only to the stupid
who know prices, sizes, ways
to squeeze through, get in,
suck up, and nothing else.
Yours is not to perfect,
but to know you can't,
and not why.

The evening shakes
and glows on the bay.
Buildings, colors, people
gild the moving sea
pours away then back
holding all in one shimmer, one
wave, as the world will not,
which slips away, then slips away.

Horse on a Fence

Horse on a Fence

We might have died by now
could be among the dead
where the numbers are greater

but for courage   course
or luck,

meeting like roads
only to divide like roads,
or regenerate,

wild,
performing the act
out loud, in the open

forgetting what
made us want to kill
made us kill
ever

believing ourselves invisible

though passion makes us
visible
even
strangely out of place
the way the present always is,
our hold on it four hooves of a horse
stopped mid-flight in a leap

standing now on a fence
between two worlds

1/1/90
Big Sur

Inflation

The brain becomes an accordion pumping its name

wheezing colors intoning personality

on pleats and keys

a monkey jumping for coins

changing

shape value and meaning day to day

JUMP you little fuck I say to the monkey JUMP for everything

praise and peanuts, sex and sleep

and every memory

you promise you'll kill for and never forget

New Hamlet

He closes his eyes

and watches the room through his eyelids

its objects and places   inches away

from sleep   choosing not to sleep   but to watch

what stays behind in the dark

and disorder—

objects and places   inside his skin

drum against it to get out but this isn't dreaming

this is looking out at looking—

when the gun goes off he'll know

he's always been a dreamer

Travel Charm

Grabs thin air

ocean   land   space

we all fear

then again

everyone you live lives

you

touch earth

which is and is not earth

touching itself

for Meghan & JP

Poppies twisted to peaks by evening light

A mourning dove coos, placid and sawing
the green wall of trees squeaking

suddenly up

the hawk hovered over
unsure of a head

snapping thistles
and yarrow
in the field
below

on the slope mission
blue butterflies bounce among lupine, paint chips,

there is no control,
there is only control.

Flits in lupine,
dies in lupine.

San Francisco Sunset 1990

An egret clenched white to pine: view from Stow Lake pavilion.

It might be better to sink this Tea Moon,
                    ignore these lacquered rafters and Taipei tones,

say things closer to earth. Loftless.

Coots shriek, a black-crowned night heron locks onto brush,
the country has gone from hell to hell to numb prosperity, sky

pinkens, vandalism is natural, all realities probable,
tightly woven berry shrubs thorn the bank.

Ducks churn, wings out, feet drag water, marking by wake.
We're all mixed together now, only one country now,
rubbed smooth across much geography.
There are too many purposes.

The Fall

It is a fear for little men

to stand up
when leaves begin   deep inside   beyond science

to change and glow it is a fear for little men to say what

will uncover them   as autumn winds

uncover trees

a fear of winds

which blow things clear

but never what is in the ear and may be tuned

to deception

the paranoid

swinging arms in lockstep beneath the trees   kissing
those they cannot scare   running from those they fear

dreaming of a friend's wife
or possessions   wanting more than they are

capable of making
or willing to work for snap snap
leaves brittle out after hot air
drops,
backdrops trembling
in slightest wind

with fear of being

uncovered,

unleafed

though death pursues the lie, centers it,
centers the wind blows leaves   breaks loose

like jazz on a blank afternoon

little men grow
in reverse

Leaf Speaks

At noon I remain confused

thinking it still dawn   sun rising right

but also setting

darkness sliding over

the ball

*

crown: root,
sky my powdered dirt

root: head,
soil my damaged light

*

What is proprietary
challenges
nature.

The leaf which falls away,
falls from its twin

Untitled

It was all stumbling
    falls and traps
I fell and falling stopped
    remembering to start remembering
again what it is about men
    not what I wish it to be—
the world is a turning
    humans cannot afford to miss—
I went to hell
    long before love itself could be tuned
to its instrument combing
    through dry grass and trees
explaining my chaos to itself
    in preparation before it struck
my head
    because it could not enter the heart
that door was closed
    when the world itself became hell
and I watched it from a hill,
    said Bashō in Nagasaki
returning to the world on a wrong day

Neo Realist

He stands on his porch in the morning stretching.
Eyes and arms vibrate, rippling blood.
Reaching into clouds, pulls but nothing happens.
Rolled morning paper a bone on the stoop he ignores.
Nothing is better than air.
Nothing more exquisite or liquid.
And all that is in it.
And all that is not.

Light

The ferry grows towards me through mottled hills.

Having driven through the ghetto to meet it

I've crossed another dark body

to stand where two midnights join,

one the fish bound sea

the other the sea of men

where darkness is a flame on the fingers.

The Pendant

Pigeon sprayed with oil
on the power line,
the earth is caked
with concrete,
dipped —
I address you   you are not low,
and because I have to
and be unembarrassed
crossing this border
placed between us
by sophistication,
by fear of being
low,
closer to death,
which we call our progress,
call the simple fact of
having to live,
call something higher
than your place,
which more and more one is
drawn to
growing tired of humans,
after petulant swats,
friends who turn
like an apple slice,
the ups and downs of vanity
lining up like the sights
of a rifle
against the heart —
I've spent my life
despising the sentimental,
distrusting the optimist inside,
trimming,
training weakness
in the blood

to turn an icy
eye upon itself,
yet now would settle
for cleaning your wings
to feel good about the world,
lift you back to shafts of air
and light,
but can only watch the shining
circle you've become,
feathers glued in
a prison
caked with earth, dipped
in this river
we love

10,000 Buddhas

Exhilarated mind flower
Fast fuck
Perdition lifter tongue-locked in the corner

The problem is that this may seem like something
you are driving through but in fact is
something
driving
you

Beginning World

Moon,
white hole in the sky
if you are living or something,
is that another white world,
white landscape spreading to infinity, a bone surface
pierced by other, bluer worlds, or red, or black,
each entered through a sky hole,
each sky with an exit or entrance.

This is about escape,
or endurance, this is about
a lack of order among men.

It's not enough to promise evolution.

Small leaves curl from small fists
into begging hands
drinking light.

Everyone has gone crazy
more than once
who understands
this hole.

The Modern World

Hops are high in Sloughhouse winding up wires,
cornfield tassels whip and snap the birds—
this same field plowed clean rises every year
after long tails of pickup and tractor dust
have settled, and black clouds of geese return
like smoke above tule fog. The scree
of red-tailed hawk above tree frog knots
on a giant oak older than everything
trails invisibly on the sky—
I've been here every year for many years
when this happens, sitting
in one black field ready for seed,
a speck on the speck, uprooted,
fully grown, terrified by beauty.

A Letter
With Franz Kline

On whitened surface,
whirlpools between pigments,
is space darker elements would die
to inhabit.

                    In that bright area directing borders.

In afternoon light you can't exist
except to bleach white back from yellowed age,
on a mountain of strokes
stacked and waiting.

                    Blood turned black against reality,
                    a paradigm beginning to surface,
                    splinter fogged beneath skin.
                    A network.

X of an outspread energy on sand.

                    The painting as a soul.

Intentional examples fail
if the subject is dilemma,
and what subject isn't—
waking up is to see
a crystal pool explode,
the hands penetrate a next membrane,
another life.

                    Franz, we are dying
                and it doesn't matter to everyone
                    who knows.

                    7/15/90

ACE 3388   7/7/92